Quick and Easy Gluten-Free Cookbook for Slow Cookers

Delicious gluten-free recipes cooked in slow cooker

Disclaimer

Contents

Introduction

If you are one of the people diagnosed with celiac disease or is suffering from gluten intolerance and if you are looking for a cookbook that will improve your condition then your search ends here. We bring you delicious and trustworthy dishes suitable for people looking for an easy gluten free diet to tackle gluten intolerances and manage weight.

We have created over 35 tempting dishes that will give you a culinary experience. There are recipes for soups, snacks and meals as well as cakes and breads. We cover recipes for outdoor eating, entertaining or for a small get together.

We have combined simple gluten free recipes. You'll discover your favourites like apple cranberry cider, sesame sriracha chicken, cuban picadillo, exotic leg of lamb and turkey rice stuffed peppers.

For parents, the cookbook offers family favorites like spaghetti squash coconut curry, meatloaf with red potatoes, smoked beef brisket, honey rosemary mustard chicken, French dip sandwich are as tasty as gluten meals.

When you get a craving for your favorite meal but don't want to spend hours in the kitchen just grab a slow cooker and this cookbook; throw in the ingredients before leaving home and come home to mouth watering cooked meal.

There are quick gluten free recipes for kids, family and guests. This book is ideal for person having

- Gluten Intolerance
- Celiac diseases
- Diabetes
- Fibromyalgia
- Autism
- Auto immune disease (lupus, rheumatoid arthritis and multiple sclerosis)

If you cook gluten free meals, "Quick and easy gluten free cookbook for slow cookers" is a lifesaver.

Tomatillo Four Bean Pork Chili

Chunks of pork shoulder slow cooked with dried beans and tomatillo

Serves 10

Cooking time: 7 Hours

Ingredients

Slow Cooker Chili (Hurst's Hambeens) and seasoning packet-15.5 oz

Water-7 cups

Onion-1

Green pepper-1

Garlic cloves-3

Pork shoulder (boneless) roast-2 lb

Drained Tomatillos-12 oz

Tomato paste-2 tbsp

Salt-1 tsp

Salt to taste

Ground pepper

Directions

- Dice onion, pepper and garlic. Trim pork of excess fat. Rinse beans and discard unwanted debris.
- Add rinsed beans into the slow cooker; pour in water. Stir in half of the seasoning mixture from the packet.
- Add onion, garlic and green pepper. Place the pork roast on the top.
- Now cover with a lid and cook for 6-7 Hours on HIGH until beans turn tender.
- After beans turn tender and pork is shreddable, turn off the heat. Take out pork; shred with two forks or use a stand mixer. After shredding place pork back into the cooker.
- Place tomatillos in the blender and blend until smooth. Add tomatillos to the slow cooker. Stir in the remaining half seasoning mixture from the packet. Add in salt, tomato paste and pepper according to your taste. Serve immediately.

Slowly Cooked "Smoked" Beef Brisket

A masterpiece recipe of smoked beef brisket rubbed with sweet and savory spices and cooked in slow cooker

Serves 10

Cooking time: 8-10 hours

Ingredients

Beef brisket (Jones Creek Beef)-3 lb

Mesquite wood chips- 1 cup

Worcestershire sauce-2 Tbsp

Liquid smoke-1 Tbsp

Garlic cloves, minced-4

Kosher salt-1 Tbsp

Black pepper-1 ½ tsp

Standard Foil (Reynolds Wrap®)

BBQ sauce

Directions

- Trim beef of extra fat. Soak wood chips for 22 minutes in water. Drain.
- Tear off a piece of Standard Foil; place at the bottom inside the slow cooker. Then press it down in the form of a slow cooker. Place the drained wood chips on the top of the standard foil.
- Tear off one more pieces of standard foil and place beef brisket on the foil. Take a sharp pointed knife and pierce beef about half inches deep. Insert garlic silvers in each cut, pushing it inside. Rub pepper and salt evenly on sides of beef brisket.
- Make a small container by bringing up sides of the wrap. Shape it into a container on which brisket will sit.
- Put this foil container along with brisket on wood chips. Pour Worcestershire sauce and liquid smoke on the brisket.
- Cook doe 8-10 Hours on LOW. Let the brisket sit on cutting board for 5 minutes. Take a sharp serrated knife and cut brisket slices.
- Brush BBQ sauce on brisket and serve.

Honey Rosemary Mustard chicken

A well seasoned chicken recipe marinated all the amazing flavours of herbs, Dijon and yellow mustard

Serves 6

Cooking Time: 6 Hours

Ingredients

1/2 onion

Garlic cloves-2

Olive oil-1 Tbsp

Crushed rosemary (dried)-1 tsp

Ground thyme-1/2 tsp

Chicken thighs (boneless, skinless)-6

Salt and pepper

Dijon mustard-2 Tbsp

Yellow mustard-2 Tbsp

Honey-1/4 cup

Tapioca (Quick cooking)-1 Tbsp

Directions

- Mince garlic and dice onion.
- Mix minced garlic and onion with thyme, rosemary and olive oil in a bowl that can be used in microwave.
- Microwave the mixture for 4 minutes. Keep stirring every 80 seconds.
- Now take chicken and put it into the bottom of the slow cooker. Sprinkle pepper and salt on them.
- Add tapioca, mustards and honey into the garlic-onion mixture and pour it over chicken in the slow cooker.
- Cover with a lid and cook for 5 Hours on LOW for 4-6 hours until the chicken looks tender and is thoroughly cooked.
- Place cooked chicken on a serving platter topped with sauce. Serve with potatoes or rice.

Exotic Shabu Shabu

A Japanese dish that looks like fondue gives you an amazing flavour. Swirl your shrimps into the simmering kombu broth and eat with the yummy sauce

Serves 4

Cooking Time: 1 Hr

Ingredients

Kombu-2 sheets

Water-2 cups

Chicken broth (fat free)-2 cups

Soy sauce-3 Tbsp

Lemon juice-1 1/2 Tbsp

Minced chives-1 tsp

Uncooked jumbo shrimp (shelled) - 1 pound

Uncooked baby bok choy-4 head

Shiitake mushroom (dried) - 2 cups

Summer squash (yellow)-2

Directions

- Half shrimps. Thinly slice mushrooms and summer squash. Rinse kombu under running water first and then place it in a bowl of cold water. Keep it submerged for 12 minutes and then drain.
- Combine broth and water in a saucepan over medium heat; add kombu. Bring the mixture to a mild simmer. After a simmer take out kombu and discard.
- Now pour the broth into a slow cooker over low heat.
- Combine chives, lemon juice and soy sauce in a bowl. Pour this sauce into 4 small bowls. Place shrimps, mushrooms and bok choy on 4 plates.
- Swirl shrimps, mushrooms and bok choy inside the simmering broth for 4-5 minutes until thoroughly cooked. You can use a skewer for this but take 1 piece at one time.
- Dip shrimps and vegetables in the chives-soy sauce mixture and eat.

Tempting Ropa Vieja

A healthy gluten free steak recipe to make for your family on a cool evening

Serves 12

Cooking time 8 Hours

Ingredients

Fat-free reduced sodium chicken broth-1 1/2 cup

Vinegar (apple cider)-1/4 cup

Ground cumin-1 Tbsp

Smoked paprika-1 tsp

Black pepper-1/2 tsp

Cayenne pepper-1/4 tsp

Flank steak (lean)-3 pounds

Red onion-2

Red pepper (sweet)-2

Fresh apple-2

Uncooked celery-3 ribs

Minced garlic clove-3

Chopped cilantro-1/2 cup

Directions

- Thinly slice celery and onion into rings. Deseed and chop red pepper. Peel, and shred apple.
- Whisk broth, black pepper, vinegar, salt, cumin, cayenne and paprika in a slow cooker. Add in the meat and submerge.
- Add onions, apples, garlic, celery and red peppers to the meat. Stir it once and make sure that the veggies are evenly distributed inside the slow cooker.
- Cook for 8 hours on LOW until thoroughly cooked
- Transfer steak onto a cutting board and shred with the help of forks. Pull it into thin strands and return it back into the cooker. Add in cilantro. It is ready to be served

Cabbage Sausage stew

A comforting and filling one-pot stew with spicy sausages, carrots, jalapeno and fire roasted tomatoes

Serves 6

Cooking Time: 7 Hrs

Ingredients

Olive Oil (Extra Virgin)

Garlic cloves-6

Onion-1

Chopped carrots-3

Chopped jalapeno-1

Shredded cabbage-1/2 head

Red potatoes -5

Salt to taste

Pepper

Fire roasted and crushed tomatoes- 28 ounce

Balsamic vinegar-¼ cup

Sage-1 teaspoon

Dried basil-1 teaspoon

Parsley-1 teaspoon

Red pepper flakes (hot)

Chicken broth (gluten free)-5 cups

Spicy sausages (gluten free)-8

Directions:

- Slice onion and chop garlic finely. Wash red potatoes and dice it.
- Cook sausages separately; cut into thick slices.
- Coat the inside of the slow cooker with olive oil and put the cooker on High.
- After 30 seconds minute, add in chopped garlic.
- Take little oil in a skillet over medium heat and add onion slices. Sauté for 3-4 minutes until soft and translucent. Now add these onions to the slow cooker.
- Add in carrots, potatoes and cabbage.
- Sprinkle with pepper and salt. Add a lot of ground pepper.
- Stir in tomatoes, sage, parsley, basil, red pepper flakes and balsamic vinegar. Stir it once.
- Now add in sausage slices.
- Pour in broth enough to submerge the ingredients.
- Cover with a lid and cook for 6 hours on high until the veggies are soft and tender.
- Adjust seasoning as per your taste before final serving.

Spinach & Mushroom Rice Lasagna

A hearty and filling lasagna with interesting veggies
layered with brown rice perfect for a chilly night

Serves 6

Cooking Time: 3 Hours

Ingredients

Marinara pasta sauce-26 oz

Diced tomatoes-14.5 oz

Mushrooms, sliced-1 cup

Fresh spinach-2 cups

Red peppers (sliced) - 1 cup

Cottage cheese-2 cups

1 egg

Mozzarella cheese-1 cup

Cooked brown rice -3 cups

Parmesan cheese (grated)-1/4 cup

Directions

- Combine tomatoes, spinach, red pepper, mushrooms and pasta sauce in a medium bowl. Divide into 3 equal portions
- Whisk egg in a bowl. Add in mozzarella and cottage cheese and mix well. Divide into 2 equal portions.
- Coat a 4 quart slow cooker with cooking spray.
- Make a layer of veggies-sauce at the bottom, then place one and a half cup of cooked brown rice over it. Spread the rice evenly over veggies.
- Spread half of the cheese-egg mixture over rice.
- Repeat layer with the remaining mixture. Top with veggies-sauce mixture.
- Cover with a lid; cook for 3 hours on HIGH until done.
- Sprinkle with grated Parmesan cheese.

Spanish Beef Olive Rice

The Spanish rice cooked along with olives and ground beef is a perfect side dish on boring weekdays

Serves: 4

Cooking Time: 3 Hours

Ingredients

Brown rice (Cover Valley) - 2 cups

All natural tomato sauce (Clover Valley)-2 (15 oz) cans

Green stuffed olives – 1 Jar

Ground beef-1 lb

1 onion

Cheddar cheese

Pepper Jack cheese

Directions

- Grate cheddar and pepper jack cheese.
- Chop 1/4th of the olives. Chop Onion
- Fry beef with a little in a medium skillet. Likewise sate onions for 2-3 minutes until translucent.
- Transfer the beef and onions into the slow cooker.
- Stir in brown rice, chopped olives, whole olives and tomato sauce.
- Cover with a lid and cook for 3 hours on high.
- Check it frequently and add water if desired.
- Top with cheese and serve.

Chicken crunch with Broccoli and Mustard

Absolutely delicious recipe of chicken cooked with

broccoli and served with cereal crumbs

Serves: 6

Cook Time: 2 hours 31 minutes

Ingredients

Olive oil (Extra-virgin) - 5 tablespoons

Chopped onion-1

Celery-2 stalks

Chopped garlic-2 cloves

Fresh thyme (chopped)-1 tablespoon

Paprika-1 teaspoon

Salt and pepper

Gluten-Free All-Purpose Flour -¼ cup

Chicken broth (reduced-sodium)-1½ cup

Heavy cream-½ cups

Dijon mustard-1 tablespoon

4 chicken breasts (boneless, skinless)-4

Instant rice-2 cups

Thawed Broccoli florets- 2 (10-ounce) packages

Rice cereal crumbs-½ cup

Directions

- Halve Celery lengthwise and cut into 1/4-inch pieces. Cut chicken breast into two inch pieces
- Marinate chicken with pepper and salt for half an hour.
- In a skillet, take two tablespoons of olive oil and heat over low-medium heat.
- Stir in onion and garlic; sauté for 2-3 minutes. Add in celery, thyme, and paprika.
- Season with little salt and pepper; stir it once. Cook for 6-7 minutes.
- Gradually sprinkle all purpose flour and stir for one minute. Take out from heat
- Stir in broth, mustard and heavy cream. Transfer the mixture to a slow cooker.
- Now place the chicken into the slow cooker; stir it once so that it is well coated with the cream sauce on all sides.
- Cook it covered for 2 hours on high.
- Now add in rice with one teaspoon of salt and cook for another 12-15 minutes.
- Add in broccoli and cook for 15 minutes more until the chicken is thoroughly cooked.
- Combine mustard, salt and cereal crumbs in a separate bowl.
- Heat olive oil in a skillet over low-medium heat. Add in cereal mixture; toast for 2 minutes.

Pepper, Beans and Tomato Chili

Intensely flavored chili combined with variety of beans, peppers and fire roasted tomatoes is sure to satisfy your taste

Serves 6

Cooking Time: 7.5 Hrs

Ingredients

Olive oil-1 Tablespoon

1 sweet yellow onion

Red bell pepper-1/2

Poblano pepper-1/2

Minced garlic-2 cloves

Tomato paste-3 Tablespoons

Chili powder-1 Tablespoon

Fire roasted and crushed tomatoes- 28 ounce

Northern beans (drained & rinsed)-15.5 ounce

Pinto beans (drained & rinsed)-15.5 ounce

Kidney beans (drained & rinsed)-15.5 ounce

Homemade vegetable broth-2 cups

Black pepper

Directions

- Deseed and chop pepper. Heat olive oil to a large skillet.
- Add in onion, poblano pepper and red bell pepper; cook for a couple of minutes.
- When onions starts turning translucent and peppers are softened add garlic. Cook for one more minute and then stir in chilli powder and tomato paste
- After 1 minute, take off from heat and transfer the mixture to a 4 quart slow cooker. Stir in roasted tomatoes, broth, beans, pepper and salt. Mix well and cook for 7 hours in Low.

Mexican Fiesta Brunch Frittata

A healthy vegan frittata made from green chile peppers, sun dried tomatoes and eggs is a great way to start your day

Serves 6

Cooking Time 3 Hours

Ingredients

Cooking spray

1 onion

1 red bell pepper

Sun-dried tomatoes-1/4 cup

Green chile peppers (fire-roasted)-14 oz can

Mexican oregano-1 tsp

9 large eggs

Skim milk-2 tsp

Low-fat Cheddar cheese (shredded)-8oz

Black pepper-1/2 tsp

Chopped cilantro and scallions for topping

Directions

- Dice onion, tomatoes and red bell pepper. Coat a slow cooker with non stick cooking spray on LOW.
- Add in onion, tomatoes, oregano, bell pepper and canned chiles. Stir it once and let heat up.
- Whisk eggs and skimmed milk together in a big bowl until smooth. Add in grated cheese and black pepper.
- Now transfer this egg mixture into the crockpot. Using a spatula, bring vegetable mixture to the top surface gently.
- Cover with a lid and cook for 3 hrs on LOW. Insert a skewer after 2 hours to check if all set. The eggs and the frittata should be set completely.
- Cut into equal portions. Top with chopped cilantro and scallions.
- Serve hot immediately.

Turkey Wraps with Sriracha in Lettuce

A flavourful combination of crunchy lettuce, carrots and meat topped with sriracha is perfect for a winter meal.

Serves 4

Cooking time: 3 hours

Ingredients

Ground turkey (lean)-1 lb

Red onion, minced -2 Tbsp

Minced garlic-3 cloves

Chinese 5 Spice-1 tsp

Gluten free Soy sauce- 2 tsp

Rice vinegar-1 Tbsp

Brown sugar-1 Tbsp

Fresh ginger, minced -2 tsp

Shredded cabbage-2 cups

1 carrot

Lettuce leaves (romaine)-8

Sriracha sauce

Directions

- Grate carrot and crumble the turkey inside the crockpot.
- Add in garlic, onion, ginger, brown sugar, rice vinegar, soy sauce and Chinese 5 Spice to the crockpot. Mix everything together.
- Cover with a lid; cook for 3 hrs on HIGH.
- Take off from heat and remove the lid. Break the meat with the help of fork or spoon. Add in grated carrot and cabbage.
- Place romaine lettuce leaves onto a serving plate. Scoop meat mixture on the leaves. Put a little amount of sriracha on each as it is very spicy.

Add in the cabbage and the carrot.

Frittata with Deli Ham, Broccoli and Cheese

Mini frittatas made with ham, broccoli florets with a special spike seasoning

Serves 6

Cooking Time: 3 Hours

Ingredients

Broccoli flowerets-3 cups

Olive oil -1 tsp

Low-fat Swiss cheese -6 oz.

Lean deli ham-6 oz.

Spike Seasoning -1 tsp.

Black pepper

12 eggs

Green onions- 2 stalks

Directions:

- Beat eggs in a bowl. Diagonally slice green onions. Cut up the broccoli into small bite-size pieces. Cut the Swiss cheese and ham into thin strips.
- Coat the insert of slow cooker with non-stick cooking spray and put it on high. Add in broccoli and sauté for 5-6 minutes.
- Layer with sautéed broccoli, deli ham and swiss cheese inside the slow cooker smoothly.
- Pour over the eggs. Season with black pepper and Spike Seasoning as per your taste.
- You can use a spatula or a fork to stir the ingredients but do it gently.
- Cook for two and a half hours on LOW until the eggs are completely set. Eggs will start leaving the sides of slow cooker.
- Frittata top wouldn't brown and will have a nice colour.
- Cut the egg frittata into equal pieces. You can arrange the pieces on a platter and top with chopped green onion.
- You can keep it refrigerated for days. Microwave the frittata at the time of eating by wrapping in a foil.

Thick Apple Pie of Steel Cut Oats

A perfect healthy creamy oats recipe with apples and dries cherries

Serves: 4-5

Cooking time: 6 Hours

Ingredients

Apples-3

Oats, Steel cut-1 cup

Water-4 cups

Pumpkin pie spice – 2 tbsp

Dried cherries-¼ cup

Directions

- Peeled apples and chop them into small pieces.
- Place the apple pieces into a 5qt slow cooker and sprinkle some pumpkin pie spice on top.
- Add in oats, raisins and 4 cups of water. Stir to mix.
- Cover with a lid and cook for 4-6 hrs.
- After 2 or 3 hours, stir it once to avoid sticking.
- Oats will turn thick and creamy.

- If it has not reached the desired thickness after taking off the heat, then cook it uncovered for some more time.
- You can store this creamy thick oats in the fridge for days.
- Reheat at the time of heating

Curry Carrot and Brown Lentil Soup

Make a great meal by cooking brown lentils & carrots in a variety of highly flavored spices and surprise your family

Serves 8

Cooking Time: 7 Hours

Ingredients

Carrots-2 lbs

Chopped onion-1

Curry powder-1/2 Tbsp

Ground cumin-1/2 Tbsp

Ginger root, grated-1 tsp

Vegetable broth-4 cups

Orange juice-1 cup

Maple syrup-1/4 cup

Harissa-1/2 tsp

Brown lentils- 1/2 cup

Salt and pepper

Chopped scallions

Directions

- Trim carrots and cut into 1-inch pieces.
- Combine onions, carrots, ginger, curry powder, cumin, orange juice and broth in a 6 qt slow cooker.
- Cover with a lid and cook for 5-6 hours on LOW.
- Uncover and add in maple syrup, lentils and harissa. Cook on HIGH for another 2 hours.
- Remove the slow cooker insert; keep it aside to cool for a couple of minutes.
- Transfer the soup to a blender; puree until smooth. Season with pepper and salt.
- Reheat and ladle soups into serving bowls; garnish with chopped scallions.

Shrimps, Squash, Kale Pepper pot

Spicy delicious one pot recipe made with shrimps, kale, peppers and butternut squash

Serves 6-8

Cooking Time: 6 Hours

Ingredients

Olive oil-1 tbsp

Onions, sliced thinly-2

Garlic, minced- 4 cloves

Ginger root, minced- 2 tbsp

Kosher salt-1 tsp

Black pepper-1 tsp

Allspice-1 tsp

Thyme leaves, dried -1/2 tsp

Bay leaves-2

Arborio rice-1/2 cup

Diced tomatoes-14-oz

Homemade chicken stock-2 cups

Butternut squash, cubed- 4 cups

Chicken thighs (boneless & skinless) - 1 lb

Chopped kale-4 cups

Uncooked medium shrimp-1 lb

Jalapeño peppers-2

Coconut milk-1 cup

Directions

- Cut chicken thighs and butternut squash into one inch cubes.
- Reserve the juice of tomatoes.
- Devein and peel shrimps and cut in halves.
- Take a medium nonstick skillet and heat olive oil over low-medium heat.
- Stir in onions; sauté for 2-3 minutes. Stir it frequently.
- When the onions starts turning translucent, add ginger, garlic, bay leaves, allspice, pepper, thyme and salt. Sauté for 2 minutes.
- Stir in rice; toss everything with a spoon.
- Add tomatoes along with the reserved juice and chicken stock; bring to a boil.
- After a boil, transfer the whole mixture into slow cooker.
- Add chicken and squash; cover with a lid and cook for 5 hrs on LOW.
- Stir the mixture once during the cooking process.
- Take 2 peppers; remove seeds and ribs from one pepper and leave the other one as it is.
- Uncover the slow cooker and add in kale little by little until all is settled.
- Add shrimps, coconut milk and jalapeno pepper.

- Cover with a lid and cook on HIGH for 15-20 minutes.
- Shrimps will turn pink and kale will be wilted. Stir it once after removing the lid. Take out bay leaves.
- Serve it immediately.

French Dip broil Sandwich with Au Jus

People pleaser sandwich of london broil cooked in slow cooker and served with au jus

Serves 4

Cooking time: 7 Hours

Ingredients:

Butter-3 tbsp

1 yellow onion

Beef broth (low sodium)-1 cup

Soy sauce (gluten free) -1/4 cup

Water-1/2 cup

Onion powder-1/4 tsp

Garlic, minced-3 cloves

Creole mustard-1 Tbsp

London broil-3 lb

Dried rosemary- one small pinch

Sea salt & pepper

Sliced mushrooms-2 cups Split sandwich rolls (gluten free) -6   Swiss cheese-6 slices

Directions:

- Cut onion in ¼ inch round slices. Arrange these slices at the bottom of the slow cooker.
- Marinate meat with onion powder, pepper and salt.
- Heat two tsp oil in a large saucepan over medium heat. Brown the meat for a couple of minutes on all sides. Turn it over and cook the other side too until browned.
- Add in beef broth, garlic, soy sauce, rosemary and mustard to the slow cooker.
- Place the browned meat onions top.
- Cook for 6 hrs on low until meat is tender and fall-apart.
- Using two forks shred meat or you can transfer the meat to a chopping board and cut into thin slices.
- Take out the onions and keep it aside. Strain juices to a measuring cup. Skim off the extra oil collecting on the top.
- Now return the beef roast, onions and juices back to the slow cooker.
- Switch the cooker to "Keep Warm" mode and keep it like that for an hour.
- Meanwhile the meat is warming, take a small saucepan and heat one tsp of oil.
- Add in mushrooms and sauté for a couple of minutes until browned. Add pepper and salt.

- Prepare the broiler and put the sandwich rolls lined with a baking sheet on the broiler.
- Toast for 40 seconds until it just begins to turn brown.
- Lay the cooked beef on sandwich rolls.
- Top with sautéed mushrooms and swiss cheese.
- Place the sandwich back to oven and heat till cheese starts to melt.
- You can top with round onion slices. Cover it with the other sandwich halves. Serve with au jus.

Tequila lime Garlic Bread

Make your own garlic bread at home with just 3 ingredients

Serves 3-4

Cooking time: 2 Hours

Ingredients

Pillsbury Pizza Dough (gluten Free)-1 tub

Garlic powder-2 tbsp

Seasoning (tequila lime)-3 tbsp

Instructions

- Keep pizza dough at room temperature for some time.
- Now place the dough in a mixer and knead for 5 minutes with the help of dough hook. It will turn soft.
- Meanwhile coat the insert of slow cooker with nonstick cooking spray evenly.
- Once the pizza dough is smooth and soft, tear off small pieces.
- Make a ball and then roll out into a bread stick. Twist a little bit and place in the slow cooker.
- Keep making bread stick with the dough until the bottom is fully occupied.

- You can also stack bread sticks one above the other but do it gently to maintain the shape.
- Sprinkle seasonings on the bread stick
- Cook for one and a half hour until all the bread sticks are completely cooked and the bottom turns dark brown.
- Turn the cooker off and remove the lid carefully. Don not let the condensation fall on bread stick.
- Take two paper towels linked together and place it over cooker opening. Return the lid.
- Let it sit for 10 minutes. It will absorb the moisture and the bread will develop a nice crust on the top.
- Take out bread and let it cool on a wire rack for some time before serving

Molten Chocolate Lava

A wonderful dessert of decadent chocolate cake with yummy choco molten core

Serves 6

Cooking time: 2 Hours

Ingredients:

Almond flour-1 1/2 cups

Baking powder-2 teaspoons

Salted butter (organic)-8 tablespoons

Chocolate chips (gluten-free)-1/3 cup

Organic sugar- 1 cup

Cocoa power (organic)-1/2 cup

Vanilla extract-1 tablespoon

Raw milk (organic) - 1/3 cup

1 organic egg yolk

Brown sugar (organic)-1/3 cup

Hot water-1 1/2 cups

Directions:

- Coat a 3 quart slow cooker with butter or oil. In a bowl mix almond flour with baking powder and keep it aside.
- Meanwhile melt butter and chocolate together in a microwave. Mix the mixture well. Add in two-third cup sugar, vanilla extract, 3tsp cocoa, egg yolk and milk. Whisk the mixture together.
- Now add in almond flour mixture; mix until everything is combined. Gradually pour this batter to the greased slow cooker.
- Combine one-third cup both of brown sugar and cocoa powder in a bowl. Add in 1/3 cup of remaining sugar. Mix well and then heat the bowl in a microwave for 1 minute until the sugar is completely dissolved. Pour this mixture on top of the batter.
- Cook for 2 hours on high until the cake is set. The top chocolate layer will be liquid. Let it cool, and then serve with whipped cream and berries.

Creamy Beef Stroganoff

Weekend special beef stroganoff with a creamy
texture served over noodles

Serves 4

Cooking time: 7 Hrs

Ingredients

Powdered milk (non fat)-2 tablespoon

Cornstarch-2 tablespoon

Garlic powder-1 tablespoon

Salt-1/2 teaspoon

Onion powder-1/2 teaspoon

Beef bouillon (Shirley J) - 1 teaspoon

Black pepper-1/8 teaspoon

Basil-1/2 teaspoon

Dried parsley-1/2 teaspoon

Dried onion-1 teaspoon

Water-1 cup

Sliced mushrooms-8 oz

Beef chuck cubed roast-1 lb

Sour cream -1/2 cup

Flour (gluten free) - 1 tablespoon

Salt, garlic powder and pepper to taste

Green onion, sliced

Directions

- Combine powdered milk, pepper, garlic powder, onion, onion powder, cornstarch, salt, parsley, basil and beef bouillon in a zipper bag. Shake to combine everything.
- Now add in meat cubes to the bag and seal it.
- Shake well until meat cubes are well coated with the mixture.
- Transfer the bag contents into a slow cooker.
- Add mushrooms and dried onions on top. Pour 1 cup water to it.
- Cover with a lid and cook for 6-7 hours on LOW till meat is tender.
- Remove the lid; stir it once. Combine flour and sour cream together in a bowl to prevent curdling.
- Add this cream mixture to the cooker.
- Adjust garlic powder, pepper and salt to taste.
- Cook the contents uncovered for 10 more minutes on HIGH.
- Serve over noodles or rice. Garnish with chopped green onion.

Marinara Sauce with Onions, Pepper and Tomatoes

A delicious spicy marinara sauce with a tint of oregano and thyme for all occasions

Serves 10

Cooking time: 8 Hours

Ingredients

POMI chopped tomato- 2 boxes (26oz)

Diced tomato, petite -2 cans (14-oz)

Tomato sauce-8 oz

1 diced onion

Garlic, minced-2 cloves

1 diced green bell pepper

Celery, diced- 1 stalk

Dijon mustard-2 tablespoon

Dried thyme-2 teaspoon

Dried oregano-1 teaspoon

Leaf-1 bay

Kosher salt-1 teaspoon

Cheese (Parmigiano- Reggiano)- 1 rind

Directions

- Keep the cheese rind aside and combine rest of the ingredients in a 6 qt crockpot.
- Cover with a lid and cook for 6 hrs on LOW.
- Stir in cheese rind; cover again. Cook for 2 more hrs on LOW.
- Adjust seasoning and add pepper and salt to taste.
- Serve hot. If you want you can keep sauce inside airtight containers in refrigerator.

Moist Meatloaf and Red Potatoes

A moist version of meatloaf cooked slowly cooked along with red potatoes is sure to bring smile on your face

Serves 7

Cooking time: 8 Hrs

Ingredients

Potatoes:

Red potatoes-8

Water-½ cup

Meatloaf:

Ground beef-1½ pounds

Instant potatoes (gluten-free)-½ cup

1 egg

Soy sauce (gluten-free)-1 tablespoon

Salt and pepper to taste

Ground sage-¼ teaspoon

Onion powder-1 tablespoon

Ground thyme-¼ teaspoon

Milk-⅓ cup

Garlic powder-⅛ teaspoon

Glaze:

Ketchup-¾ cup

Brown sugar-2 tablespoons

Nutmeg-⅛ teaspoon

Directions

- Peel the potatoes; cut them into one inch size chunks.
- Put the potatoes chunks in the slow cooker greased with cooking spray or oil. Add water to it.
- In a bowl combine the ingredients of the meatloaf. You can use a stand mixer but keep the speed on low.
- Put the meatloaf over potatoes; give it an oval shape or any shape you want to cover the potatoes chunks.
- In a bowl combine the ingredients of glaze. Spread the glaze evenly over meatloaf.
- Now cover with a lid and cook for 8 hrs on low until the potatoes and meatloaf are thoroughly cooked.

Beef-Mushroom Gravy

Delicious and easy to make mushroom gravy with
good quality stew meat cooked in beef broth

Serves 6

Cooking time: 4 Hours

Ingredients

Stew meat-2 pounds

Beef broth-2 cups

Arrowroot starch-2 tablespoons

Diced mushrooms-6 ounces

1 onion, chopped

Garlic, minced-2 cloves

Coconut oil-1 tablespoon

Salt to taste

Ground Pepper

Directions

- Whisk arrowroot starch with broth in a bowl until smooth.
- Pour this mixture into a medium saucepan over medium heat.
- Keep stirring the sauce for a couple of minutes until it thickens. When it starts bubbling, take off from the heat.
- Heat oil in another small sauté pan and add onions to it over medium-high heat.
- Sauté for 2-3 minutes until the onion is translucent. Add in garlic; cook for 1 more minute.
- Add the sautéed onion-garlic and mushrooms to the starch-broth sauce.
- Season with pepper and salt and stir it well.
- Now place the meat to the bottom of the slow cooker insert.
- Pour the thick creamy sauce over meat and stir well to combine.
- Cook for 4 hrs on High until the stew meat turns soft and tender.
- Mix well after taking off from heat. Serving over noodles or rice.

Cube Steaks with Soy Mushrooms

Mouth watering cube steaks cooked with a lot of mushrooms in the slow cooker

Serves 6

Cooking time: 4 Hours

Ingredients

Steaks-6 cube

1 onion, sliced

Soy sauce (gluten free)

Seasoned salt

Garlic, minced-2 cloves

Sliced mushrooms

Corn starch

Directions

- Put onion slices at the bottom of the slow cooker. Add ½ cup water to the slow cooker.
- Put some soy sauce, garlic, seasoned salt and mushrooms on each steak.
- Arrange steaks inside the slow cooker in layers.
- Cover with a lid and cook for 4 hrs on High.

- Take out the onions, fatty bits and steaks from the broth.
- Whisk 1 ½ tsp of cornstarch with 1 cup of water. The water should be cold.
- Pour this mixture into the slow cooker and whisk together everything.
- Switch the slow cooker to HIGH while whisking. You can do this in a skillet on the gas stove.
- Bring the mixture to a boil; take off from the heat.
- Pour this juicy thick broth over steaks and onions.
- Serve hot.

Curried Chuck Roast and Carrots

Curry powder gives a spicy flavour to tender chuck roast cooked with carrots, onions and tapioca

Serves 8

Cooking time: 4 Hours

Ingredients

Chuck roast – 4 pounds

2 onions

10 medium carrots

Bay leaves-2

Curry powder-1 tablespoons

Beef broth-1 cup

Ground ginger-1½ teaspoons

Salt

Black pepper-½ teaspoon

Minute tapioca-¼ cup

Directions

- Pell onions and carrots.
- Chop onions into thick slices and put them inside the slow cooker of capacity 6 quart.
- Similarly cut carrots into one inch thick pieces and place them over onions in the slow cooker.
- Place the bay leaves over on carrots.
- In a bowl combine tapioca, ginger, curry powder, beef broth, pepper and salt.
- Pour half of the mixture over veggies in the slow cooker
- Place chuck roast on the top. Pour the other half of the broth over chuck roast.
- Cover with a lid and cook for 4 hrs on HIGH until the roast is cooked through.
- Remove the meat from the slow cooker and turn the slow cooker on HIGH.
- Let the vegetable cook for some more time. Serve meat and veggies in a platter.

Moroccan Spicy Chickpea Stew

A healthy chicken stew recipe featuring rich spices like coriander, turmeric and paprika perfect for a cold winter

Serves 8

Cooking time: 8 Hours

Ingredients

Cooking spray

Ground turkey (93% lean)-1.3 lb

Olive oil (extra virgin)-1 tbsp

1 chopped yellow onion

Garlic, chopped- 2 cloves

Chopped poblano pepper-3 tbsp

Diced carrots-1 cup

Diced celery-1 cup

Petite tomatoes, diced -28 oz can

Chick peas, drained-2 (15 oz) cans

Low sodium chicken broth (99% fat free)-2 cups

Turmeric-2 tsp

Paprika-2 tsp

Coriander-1 tsp

Bay leaves-2

Red pepper flakes, crushed -1/2 tsp

Coarse salt-2 tsp

Chopped fresh parsley-2 tbsp

Directions:

- Take a nonstick skillet and coat it with cooking spray. Place the skillet over low-medium heat.
- Add in ground turkey and cook for 10-15 minutes.
- Take two forks and break up turkey in the skillet and then transfer to the slow cooker.
- Add olive oil to the nonstick skillet over high heat.
- Stir in onions, carrots and peppers; sauté for 5-6 minutes until soft.
- Stir in garlic and celery and cook for additional 2 minutes.
- Transfer the ingredients of the skillet to slow cooker. Stir in chick peas, tomatoes, broth and spices. Stir well to combine everything.
- Cover the cooker and cook for 6-8 hrs on LOW.
- Uncover and discard bay leaves
- Ladle into serving bowls and top with fresh chopped herbs.

Slow Cooked Braised Cabbage

Cabbage slow cooked with wine, sweet onion and caraway seeds is a perfect side dish on weeknights

Serves 6

Cooking time: 6 Hours

Ingredients:

Green cabbage-1 head

1 sweet onion, sliced

Garlic, chopped- 4 cloves

Bacon fat, melted-1/4 cup

Wine - 1/2 cup

Smoked sea salt

Caraway seeds

Apple cider vinegar

Directions:

- Take a 6 qt slow cooker and add bacon fat at the bottom.
- Turn the switch to HIGH and add onion to it.
- Cut off the hard stem of cabbage end.

- Divide the cabbage in 12 wedges with the core attached.
- Arrange the cabbage wedges in layers inside the slow cooker.
- Pour wine over cabbage. Add in salt to taste and caraway seeds.
- Cover and cook for 1 hr on HIGH.
- Check it frequently; stir the wedges gently so that all pieces are cooked through completely.
- Add more fat or wine if required.
- Continue cooking the cabbage for 4-5 more hrs on high
- Drizzle with apple cider vinegar or balsamic vinegar.
- Adjust seasoning with pepper and salt.
- Serve immediately or store in refrigerator. Reheat at the time of eating.

Exotic Leg of Lamb

A wonderful recipe of lamb leg cooked in an exotic spice rub is sure to fulfil the expectations of your taste bud

Serves 6

Cooking time: 3 Hours

Ingredients

Leg of lamb-5 pound

Your favourite sauce

Mustard Rub:

Olive oil-2 tbsp

Dijon mustard-2 tbsp

Dried rosemary- 4 tbsp

Oregano or thyme

Coarse sea salt-1 tbsp

Black pepper, cracked

Garlic, crushed- 2 cloves

Directions:

- Mix everything except lamb in a medium bowl.

- Rub this mixture over lamb leg that is thawed
- Let the marinade sit for 2 hrs at room temperature or keep in the fridge for a night.
- Take out of the fridge and let it come to room temperature.
- Place the leg in the slow cooker and cook for 2-3 hours on LOW until the meat thermometer reads 120°F(rare roast) or 130° F (medium roast)
- Take it out and let sit for 10-15 minutes
- Cut in to slices and serve with your favorite sauce.

Picadillo of heart, liver, and kidney

Spiced vegetable and beef hash prepared in a traditional way with kidney, liver and heart

Serves 4

Cooking time: 8 Hours

Ingredients

Ground beef-3 lbs

Ground organ meat mix (heart, liver, kidney)-1 lb

Diced onion -4 cups

4 green bell peppers

4 tomatoes

Pitted olives with brine (Spanish manzanilla)-5 1/2 oz jar

Garlic, minced-8 cloves

Ground cumin-2 tsp

Dried oregano-2 tsp

Bay laurel, dried -5 leaves

Unrefined salt-1 tsp

Black pepper-1 tsp

Ground cinnamon-1/2 tsp

Ground cloves-1/4 tsp

Fresh cilantro-1 handful

Directions

- Deseed tomatoes and pepper. Dice all the vegetables like tomatoes, bell peppers and onions.
- Mix cloves, cinnamon, garlic, bay leaves, pepper, oregano, cumin and salt in a bowl.
- Now add the veggies to the slow cooker and fill up to half of the cooker. Then add in spice mixture over the vegetables.
- Add in olives along with brine. You can chop olives or put it whole as you desire.
- Stir the ingredients once.
- Now add meat into the slow cooker. Break the organ meat into small pieces using a fork. The pieces should be the size of grapes.
- Stir it to combine meat with spices and veggies.
- If you have organ mix then add now and mix again.
- Add in the remaining meat (ground beef) to the slow cooker and mix again
- Cook for 7-8 hrs on LOW
- Uncover and stir with a big spoon. Break up meat clumps cooked together in the process. Don't worry about the flavour. The flavour is same as it is of the browned meat
- Serve with white rice or cauliflower-rice
- Keep it in freeze for days and reheat before eating

Honey Sesame Sriracha chicken

Sweet savory & spicy version of chicken made in honey, sriracha and topped with sesame seeds

Serves 5

Cooking time: 3.5 Hours

Ingredients

Chicken breasts (boneless and skinless)-1-1.5 lbs

Honey-2 tbsp

Sesame oil-1 tsp

Rice vinegar-1 1/2 tbsp

Paleo Sriracha-1/2 tsp

Tamari- 3 tbsp

Tomato paste-2 tbsp

Water-2 tbsp

Arrowroot starch-2 tsp

Garlic, minced - 1 tsp

Yellow onion, minced -1/2 cup

Minced jalapeno-1 tsp

Sesame seeds

Scallions

Lime wedges

Directions

- Combine honey, tomato paste, rice vinegar, tamari, sesame oil and sriracha in a bowl.
- Deseed jalapeno if you want it less spicy otherwise leave it. Mince jalapeno and garlic clove; chop onion
- Add minced jalapeno, garlic and onion to the bowl. Mix everything together.
- Combine starch and water together to form a smooth paste and dissolve any clumps formed.
- Add the starch mixture to bowl. Stir it well.
- Arrange chicken breasts pieces inside the slow cooker
- Pour the sauce in the bowl gently all over chicken breast. Make sure that chicken is covered fully with the sauce.
- Cover and cook for 3.5 hrs on HIGH or 6 hrs on LOW
- The chicken will be very tender and soft after it is cooked through.
- Take two forks and break the chicken pieces
- Stir it with a big spoon.
- You can either eat it alone or serve it over quinoa, rice or noodles
- Garnish with scallions, lime wedges and sesame seeds.

Spicy Turkey-Rice Stuffed Peppers

Turkey, rice and tomatoes make a delicious filling for these colourful stuffed peppers

Serves 3

Cooking time: 5 Hours

Ingredients

3 multi-colored bell peppers

Uncooked rice-1/3 cup

Ground turkey-1/2 lb

Chopped onion-3/4 cup

Garlic, minced- 2 cloves

Tomatoes, diced – 1 cup

Dried basil-1/4 teaspoon

Oregano-1/4 teaspoon

Salt to taste

Pepper-1/2 teaspoon

Allspice- 1 small pinch

Fresh basil, minced -1 tbsp

Pepperjack cheese, grated -1/2 cup

Basil leaves

Directions

- Chop onions. Finely mince garlic. Chop basil.
- Combine together garlic, tomato & its juice and onion, garlic in a large bowl. Tomato juice is necessary for retaining moisture in the stuffing.
- Add seasonings and basil to the bowl. Mix the ingredients well.
- Add raw rice and meat
- Deseed peppers by cutting the top circular part and taking out seeds. Rinse
- Peppers are now ready to fill in the stuff.
- Take a small spoon and fill the meat-rice mixture into the deseeded peppers.
- Don't fill it completely. Leave some space at the top for rice to expand. Avoid breaking of the peppers.
- Now arrange these peppers in a slow cooker.
- Add 1 tsp of water at the bottom of the cooker and your peppers won't stick or burn. The peppers itself releases moisture.
- Grate pepperjack cheese and sprinkle over stuffed peppers inside the slow cooker.
- Cover with a lid and cook for 5 hrs on HIGH.
- After the peppers are done, they will look a little wrinkly.
- Finish off with more grated cheese.
- Put basil leaves on top and serve.

Roasted Pepper Soup with Garlic Basil Oil

A yummy tomato soup drizzled with seasonings in
olive oil and balsamic vinegar

Serves 6

Cooking time: 1 Hour

Ingredients

Olive oil-2 tbsp

Diced white onion-1

Garlic, minced-3 cloves

Red peppers, roasted-12 oz

Drained sun dried tomatoes-8 oz

Vegetable stock-4 cups

Dried thyme-1 tsp

Dried oregano-1 tsp

Basil leaves-1 cup

Olive oil-1/2 cup

Garlic-1 clove

Pepper

Directions

- Sauté onion in a greased saucepan over high heat. Cook for 3 minutes until translucent.
- Add garlic and cook for 1 minute. Transfer to a slow cooker.
- Stir in tomatoes, spices, peppers and stock into the slow cooker. Let it simmer for an hour on LOW.
- While the soup simmers, take 1 clove of garlic, black pepper and basil to the food processor.
- Stir in half cup olive oil to the processor and pulse until smooth.
- Pour soup from the cooker into a blender and make a smooth puree. Ladle soups into bowls. Drizzle over basil oil in each bowl.

Spaghetti Squash Coconut Curry

A low ingredient gluten-free dish of spaghetti squash
cooked in coconut milk and red curry paste

Serves 6

Cooking time: 4 Hours

Ingredients

Spaghetti squash- 3 pounds

Coconut milk (full fat)-1 can

Water -1/4 cup

Red curry (Thai Kitchen) paste- 2 Tbsp

Garlic -4 cloves

Chopped cilantro

Directions

- Halve spaghetti squash with a knife (preferably serrated one).
- Remove the seeds of the squash halves. Save the seeds for other use.
- Take a fork and pin 4 holes on top of squash halves.
- The coconut milk should be at room temperature and well shaken.
- Pour water and coconut milk to the slow cooker.
- Stir in garlic cloves and curry paste into the slow cooker.
- Stir with a spoon until everything is well combined.
- Place poked squash halves into the coconut mixture with the cut side facing downwards.
- Cover with a lid and cook for 4 hrs on LOW.
- Take out squash from slow cooker with the help of a big fork.
- Place the squash halves in a bowl.
- Mash up the garlic cloves in the curry
- Add the coconut curry from the slow cooker over squash.
- Top with chopped cilantro and serve.

Slow cooked Brownies

Homemade fresh brownies that is perfectly satisfying
and decadently rich

Serves 10

Cooking Time: 4 Hours

Ingredients

Almond flour-2 cups

Coconut sugar -1 cup

Cocoa powder, unsweetened -3/4 cup

Baking powder-2 tsp

Baking soda-2 tsp

Salt-1 tsp

2 eggs

Coconut milk (full-fat), unsweetened -1/2 cup

Butter-1/2 cup

Vanilla extract-2 tsp

Brewed coffee -1/3 cup

Directions

- Melt the butter by microwaving for 10 seconds.
- Coat the insert of slow cooker with melted butter.
- Mix almond flour, cocoa powder, baking powder and baking soda in a bowl.
- Whisk eggs in a medium bowl.
- Add in melted butter, coconut milk, coconut sugar and brewed coffee and mix well with a spoon.
- Add in the dry ingredients little by little to avoid any lump formation; stirring continuously
- Finally add salt and vanilla extract. Stir to form a smooth batter.
- Cook for 5 hrs on LOW. Check with a skewer.
- After it is done, cool for half an hour. Using a large spoon, scoop out brownie balls.
- Drizzle with caramel glaze.

Tomato and Balsamic Onion Roast

A simple and savory balsamic pot roast cooked with sun dried tomatoes in beef broth

Serves 4

Cooking Time: 4 Hours

Ingredients:

1 beef roast

3 sweet onions

Sun-dried tomatoes-1 cup

Salt & pepper-1 Tbsp

Garlic powder-1 Tbsp

Lard -2 Tbsp

Balsamic vinegar-1/2 cup

Beef broth-1.5 cups

Directions:

- Marinate beef roast with garlic pepper and salt. Leave it for 15 minutes.
- In a hot skillet, sear the roast in lard.
- Sear both sides of the beef for 4-4 minutes until browned.
- Now cut onions into slices and place them at the bottom of the slow cooker.
- Place browned beef over onion slices.
- Cook tomatoes separately in one cup of water till soft. Purée in a blender.
- Pour the tomato puree into the slow cooker over beef.
- Pour in balsamic vinegar and beef broth.
- Cover with a lid and cook for 4 hrs on high until meat is thoroughly cooked.
- Take out meat and place them on a cutting board. Cut into slices.
- Keep cooking the liquid in the slow cooker till it reduces to half.
- Drizzle this thick liquid over beef
- Serve meat with cooked onion and thick sauce.

Apple Cranberry Cider

Warm apple cider cooked with orange pieces, apple, cranberries, with a tint of flavourful spices

Serves 4

Cooking Time: 6 Hours

Ingredients

Apple juice-6 cups

Cranberry juice-3 cups

Honey-1/4 cup

Fresh cranberries-1/2 cup

1/2 orange

1/2 apple (Granny Smith)

Fresh ginger- 5 thick slices

Cinnamon sticks-4

Whole cloves 10

Ground allspice-1/4 tsp

Ground nutmeg-1/8 tsp

Directions

- Pour apple and cranberry juices in the slow cooker
- Add cinnamon sticks & cranberries. Cut apple into thin slices.
- Cut half orange into thin slices and peel its rind using peeler.
- Add orange slices, apple slices and orange rind into the slow cooker.
- Cut fresh ginger into 5 long thick slices so that you can remove it in the end
- Add ginger pieces into the cooker.
- Add in nutmeg, cloves and allspice. Stir it once.
- Cook for 6 hrs on LOW.
- Serve or keep refrigerated in jar.

Conclusion

Everyone including gluten intolerant person wants a quick meal at the end of a busy day. This book is a nice collection of delicious and popular slow cooked gluten free meals. Now you don't have to eat boring food.

This book has all the wonderful gluten free recipes that you have dreamt of. These enticing recipes don't sacrifice on flavor or texture and easily fit in your busy schedule. If you are planning to cut down on gluten in your diet, then this book is all you need.

16621631R00054

Made in the USA
Middletown, DE
18 December 2014